Sailing to Redemption Throu

WHITE WHALE

FRANK PREM

Publication Details

Title: White Whale
ISBN: 978-1-925963-97-7 (pbk)
ISBN: 978-1-925963-99-1 (e-bk)

Published by Wild Arancini Press
Copyright © 2024 Frank Prem
All rights reserved:

No part of this publication may be reproduced, stored in a retrieval system, or transmitted in any form or by any means, electronic, mechanical, photocopying, recording or otherwise, without prior written permission from the publisher and author.
A catalogue record for this book is available from the National Library of Australia.

Book cover design and formatting services by WildAranciniPress.com

Contents

Who knew? The whale was me. Always me.

About White Whale

White Whale came to life as a detour on my journey through T. S. Eliot's The Waste Land, when I found myself, unexpectedly, engaged in a story about a whale, out of its element and dying. I then discovered that it was not alone.

Ahab the mariner and Moby the white whale inhabiting a desert ocean together, and one of them was dying.

What evolved to become a kind of spiritual wandering and ultimately, a journey in search of a form of redemption that can only come about through transformation of the soul.

White Whale is, I think, a glorious story that reaches beyond an expanse of sand and the passing of a stranded cetacean.

FP

2023

Prelude

so many seas (such vast deaths)

white
on white

the colour
null

a pallid cetacean rests –
stranded –
on the bed
of a blonde
desert

all the while
circled
by a motorized dinghy
captained by a bearded mariner
wearing a –
predominantly blue –
cap of command
and
sharply trimmed –
predominantly *black* –
beard

as he ploughs
through the sand
the mariner is shouting –
encouragements
and endearments –
to the whale

come moby

swim

dive
below the surface
and
sound your song

dive
you beautiful
pale fool

dive

if you languish
you will surely
die
and that
is not acceptable to me

swim
damn you

become
of-the-sand

your appointed task
is to be hunted
by me

I demand
you swim

the whale blinks

rotates
an enormous
blue
cetaceous eye
to follow the motion
and wake
of the little boat –
of
its old nemesis

performing agitated arcs
and circles
through the sand

urging

always urging

but
the whale
is tired

weary of the coarse-grains
of spiracle-fouling irritation
that hamper
breathing

of the constant crusting
of ever-weeping
lachrymals

and
of this dry air
filled with powdered dust
and the sound

of that wretched man
beseeching

as though
it is not
enough
to have been marooned
so unexpectedly

or to be overtaken
by this
un-fathomable
new
not-water

a fluke twitches
responding
to the whale's distress
with
just the suggestion
of a tail
loaded with sand

and flung . . .

to achieve
the swamping
of a small boat . . .

just to show that old salt
that a pale whale
is not
ever
helpless

merely . . .

biding

in the end
though
the whale does
nothing

it waits –
a long cetacean
moment –
for
a propitious time

to dive

to overturn
the absurd dinghy
and
the blusterous mariner
both

to exploit the confusion
and sudden intensity
of disturbance

until then
though . . .

until then . . .

it sends a
ripple
along the length
of a drying flank

to disturb the ticks
and the fleas
and the sand flies . . .

the wretched seagulls
here
so far
from salted water

it listens
to the sounds
of the sailor
and his motorized boat

and prepares
to die

one single
white granule
at a time

encouragement (at an ending)

the mariner
is frantic

there is
a desperation
that accompanies the circling
of his little boat

an end
imminent
to his questing pursuit

he is not
prepared
to acknowledge it

not prepared
to accept

he exhorts
again

part shout

part
encouragement

part abuse

invective
in all the shades
that he can imagine
or conjure

there is no question
from him
about how he comes –
how *they*
come –

to be in the heart
of a barren
desert

he with his little
motorboat

the whale
beyond all hope
of water

the *how*
seems immaterial
in the face
of the helplessness
that it causes

the inability
to take action

to pursue
or
to flee

to remedy
or resolve

a shallow disturbance
of air –
barely visible –
at the spiracle
tells him
that an end
is near

he shouts
another
encouragement

spectacle (in the desert arena)

the birds –
gleaming white
their feathers –
are untroubled

do not appear
to notice the heat
nor the flies

the biting
insects
that infest the entire expanse
of sand

they are focused
exclusively now
on this –
soon-to-be –
carcass

so
out of its element
that it attracts them
in clouds

flies
midges
lizards
scorpions
slithering snakes
and
hopping mice

all have come
to bite and drink
and feed

to lay their eggs

to bypass

and to stare at
in naked
curiosity

briefly

it must be
briefly
for the sun is ever-ready
to broil
the unwary

some
of the passing
spare a moment
to stare
also
at the distraught man

as he
silently
weeps

white smiles (remora scatter)

the fin
of a great-white
breaks the surface

slices
through the yellow-white
undulations
of the sprawl
of sand

it is a
sleek
creature

~

the huge white
cetacean
is exhausted

a puff of dust
and periodic
faint whistling
are all the signs of life
it has left
to manifest

it is aware –
now –
that it is being circled
and sized

how not?

yet
it remains placid
in mood

resigned
to fate

it has seen off
the mad sailor
but
but in the end
even the unending battle
must cease
and
it bears the knowledge
that truth
comes
at the last

there is no longer
any need
for self-deception
or
for lies

~

the shark
continues
to circle

nearer

it is not
an unkind creature
and
in fact
it does not exist
in *that* sort
of world

it knows the whale
is a living thing

and it knows
too
the taste of death
simultaneously diffusing
through the sands

there will be more
sharks
and a savage feast

~

little trails
of dust
hover in the air

gradually merging
into a brown smear
above and around
the ailing creature

the cloud thickens
with each circumnavigation
by the shark

and with each shallow
expulsion
through the blowhole

~

is it worth the effort
to speak?

a valid question –
fair –
for both prey
and predator

one last chance
to set the record
straight . . .

an opportunity
to clarify
innocent intentions . . .

no
no

~

a trembled ripple
runs down the flank
of the last
white whale

the shark
draws back its lips
in a rictus smile
that is all teeth

arrows in
through the shushing sand
to take a first bite
from the
soon-to-be
carcass

remora
scatter

the desert
rolls on

white sand white whale white beard white bone (all end all end)

there is no
ocean of sand
remaining

time
has claimed it . . .

moved it on
like a policeman
performing crowd control
at the site
of a calamity

an apparition –
it is the old mariner –
is perched
within a skeletal fold
of bone

the whitened remains
of what must have been
a very large whale

the skeleton
as a whole
gleams
in sunlight

its entirety
exposed
in the absence
of the sustaining element

white sand

there is music
in the air

funereal
and high in pitch
for the wind
plays
among the bones

in a pinch
anything
will serve
as a tool

an instrument

there is
a vocal accompaniment

a rise and fall
within the song
of a white-bearded sailor
weeping

he is crying
for
so many things

his foolish past

and belated present

the loss
of his only companion
through so many
uncertain years

realization
at the end
that he was not –
had *never* been –
alone

not *truly*
alone

not while the whale
lived –
even there
and then
in the terrible sand ocean
of the desert

the bones
are unmoved
and unmoving
in the dry air
that surrounds this
monument
to unreasoning pursuit

and compulsion

but
at the touch
of the first teardrop
on the calcifying
cetaceous skull
something
is released

some shadow

of
a whale that was
shivers
the light

and swims

the old sailor
is unaware

looking too deeply
into
his own grief
but
a spirit
has been released
and
is gone

White Whale

nemesis (do I yet know you)

when
did it happen?

he ponders
as he walks

it is almost unbearably hot
in his oilskin
and sou'wester

waterproof trews
and deck boots

when
did the ocean
become a desert . . .

and
how long after that
did it become
incapable
of keeping a boat
afloat?

when did it change
to mere dust . . .

to sand?

sometime –
he thinks –
around when the whale
stopped swimming

stopped living

stopped filling the role
of *spiritual brother*
to a nautical obsessive

gradually . . .

eventually

the whale
turned to bone
and
his boat
became desiccated timbers

protruding ribs
half buried
beneath a rising dune
and
an almost perfect match

just like a cetacean
and its mariner

beneath
the overbearing sun
it has become necessary
to walk
though
a destination
is less clear

in any case . . .

in the desert ocean
of the end of your life
one road
is much like
another
and arthritic bones
will allow no peace

no rest

no comfort

how long –
he wonders –
before he crosses
his own tracks
and meets the knowledge
that he
has become lost?

soon enough
soon enough

he sustains himself
in his wanderings
by reliving mental images
of himself . . .

harpoon in hand
and with the pursuit running
hot

the whale-sounds –
tantalizingly close –
just out of reach

as always

the realization
of kinship
with that mighty creature
has come slowly

and with a great wash
of unease

he misses
his white nemesis
now
almost more than
he can bear

grief or glee (a whipping)

there is a point
where
even the sand
must end

even the solitude
of *sand*
comes to an end

replaced
by rocky tors
of cutting isolation . . .

desolation
more like

the wind
sneers
a perverted whale song
pitched high . . .

then
low . . .

then
simply shrieking

until his ears
are filled
with a kind
of madness

the whale is gone
the whale
is gone

> *why*
> *did he seek*
> *to kill the whale?*

> *why*
> *did he stop?*

> *when*
> *did it become*
> *imperative*
> *that he save it?*

the whale
is gone

yet it inhabits
his mind
inflicting mental cuts
and abrasions

bruises
with every new thought

sometimes
the song sounds
like derision
directed at himself
by the ghost of the white creature

a true haunting
brought on by loneliness
and grief

an awareness
of a personal role
in the grounding
of the white beast

the sound
of his weeping
is swallowed whole
and carried away
almost before
he hears it
himself

there is a
long-lingering glee
whipping in the tail
of the wind

ponders the mariner (but still the sun burns)

what if they had remained
where they were
while the ocean
was still composed
of water?

what if
he had not pursued
so relentlessly . . .

though *that*
was not
a one-sided thing

for he knew
in his heart
that he had been
goaded

and
what if
he had realized
the true nature
of that pursuit
much earlier?

if he had aligned –
perhaps –
the two mirror glasses
to establish
a single image

the true
image

and what if . . .

and what
if

it could all
be different
if . . .

but the changes –
as they came –
had been subtle
things

the transformation
from salt and water
to furnace
and to sand . . .

imperceptible

until
they were the only
truth
and water
merely a reference point
in history

could it
have been
different?

he was unable
to decide

but days passed
while he pondered

and the sun
continued
to burn

a splash (of whale water)

from a distance
the two figures seem . . .

equal

in size
and in proportion

it is a matter
of perspective

they are
a pair

perhaps . . .

a couple

it is only
as they draw closer
that the senses
protest

for one seems vast
now

vast and white
and luminescent

the other
is small

smaller than he appeared
from a distance

he seems
unaware
of his companion

lost
in his thoughts

while the great leviathan
keeps pace

occasionally
leaps
into the air

seeming
to splash mystical water
as it lands

a joyous freedom
unbounded

the old man
wipes salty water
from his cheek
unaware
that he weeps
the whale's ocean

the wave (the one wave)

it is said
amongst mariners
that
out on the sea
there is a wave

one wave

that is the incarnation
of your name
and spirit

a wave that holds
your destiny

if you see it
you are . . .

    doomed

    destined

    required

you must
be
what the wave declares
you to be

the mariners
hold this tale
to be
truth

and so . . .

fate
works its tricks

~

he had seen it
when on the peak
of a swelling wave
in his boat

a distant brother wave
rose
at the same moment

equally mountainous

risen up
out of the bed
of the ocean

and in the translucent heart . . .

in the aquamarine
of water and spray
and froth
and turmoil

he had spied
the white whale

a glimpse –
no more –
of that giant
majesty

held aloft
by the wave
as though . . .

as though
an afterthought

without substance

the mariners eyes
were transfixed
and he could not stop
seeing it

even after
the wave had subsided

after the waters
had calmed

there was nothing
else
in all the world

and that world
had become
pursuit

even now
he seeks the creature
in his mind

drowning perhaps (never alone)

an old theory
of schizophrenia
had the mind severing
into two

another
described a split
away
from reality

voices
from *without*

voices
from *within*

never alone

never at peace

yet some have spoken
of their experience
as
companionship

familiarity
with their own
personal demons
providing a kind of
chattering comfort

a life
lived
with ghosts inside

~

the man walked
alone

his animation
a suggestion
of active involvement
in conversation

gunshot bursts
of laughter

    ha
    ha
    ha

grimaces
and gesticulations

alone

not alone

he walked
as though
drowning

to rest (without fever)

the shape
of a thought
is a swirling thing

smoke
and mist

opacity enough
to obscure

yet
the thought remains
within
the shroud

it whistles

and
it sings

the sound –
almost –
of a sanity
belonging in the past

of wets

and deeps

and eagerness
and
of joy . . .

emerging
from the white fog
comes
the white thought

there is
a moment
of recognition

.

.

.

a moment of peace
inside
an over-fevered
mind

enough
to close eyes

to rest

the shepherd guides (a flipper step)

come

a flipper touch

come

guidance from . . .

a shepherd?

there is
a way

it is –
as it has always been –
forward

beyond sand
rocky crag

beyond life . . .

and death

forward

and the path
is

a single step

one more
and . . .

a single step

but
not alone

no
no more alone

turmoil calms . . .

    another step

a clearer
mind

    another step

beyond mountains
now . . .

    another step

beyond
alien lands

a flipper
guides
for another step

the shepherd comes
and you
are two

for

    another step

sing (for once we were)

oooo-weee-ooo-ooo

oooo-weee-ooo-ooo

let us sing

raise
our voices high

let us sing
a song
of sweet
sad sorrow

for the loss –
the *physical* loss –
is real

and the emptiness
is all
around

let us sing
for in our minds
we are
still
one
and one

in our minds
the harpoon
and
the salt water

oooo
oooo-weee-ooo-ooo

ocean
deep

oooo-weee-ooo-ooo

water
wide

oooo

let us leave
the storm behind

oooo

sing
the song of

once
we were

there is no crowd (within a fog)

paths open

there is no
crashing

no jostling

the one
that is dazed
progresses

crowds part
as though
he is a presence . . .

has
a presence

he
is unaware

unseeing

stepping
through pallor
as insubstantial
as mist

in truth
this could be
another land

a different
place

for what is occupied
is a room
in his mind

a retreat
from all
cacophony

within
and without

lost
yet . . .

perhaps
on a path
to finding

the fog rolls on
leading
each footstep

edges shaved (throbbing on)

nothing lasts

even fog will clear
at times

long enough
to allow a glimpse
away
to the distance

the far-off
forever

it is bleakness –
like a blanket –
covering emptiness

and enough
to bring forth
a sigh

a dissent
and
a dejection

but there is a song
still
being sung . . .

*some*where

it rises
like a feeling –
a sensation
of warmth –
that begins
at the bones

from the earth
and up
into the man

he is unconscious
of it

but
is somehow minded
of the sea

of the sound
of gulls
calling

it does not last
of course
for the fog descends
to enshroud
and still all sensation
again

to dim his wit

and shave the edges
of his passion

dull and raw
and
throbbing

he walks on

an instinctive
direction

immured
to his own pain

oblivious

a swim light (an ocean destiny)

there is a light
shining
from just over the hill

a glow that haloes
through the sky

he knows
what it is

destiny

destination

an *answer* . . .

or
perhaps just another
question

it does not matter

he knows
the light
is there
to draw him on

he can imagine
swimming
out to sea

on an ocean
of that light

ground sung (the ocean)

the whale
has no concerns
about its new
metaphysical
state

it is not a believer
in ghosts
or spirits

alive
it was a creature
of the moment

of salt water
and krill

deep songs
and narrow light

and
of the mariner

it too
was crested
by its own version
of the one wave

it too was
required
to respond

twined

entwined

to the man
and his foolish
harpoon obsession

now
it remains
a creature of the moment

though the moment
is of air

and the creature
somewhat ethereal

it does not
feel
the torment
of the man –
once a mariner –
as he shifts and changes
within himself

it is merely . . .

there

almost
of him
but . . .

not

it sings
quietly
a whale song . . .

a comfort

it is a sound
that communicates
as feeling

rising into a body
through its boots

travelling through earth
that is now
the ocean

a feeling foreseen (in the foam)

the orb
is clear

the orb wears
white caps . . .

riding
upon the water

tiny creatures
swarm
like an orchestrated troupe
of darkened dancers

they are many

you
are there but . . .

I do not
recognize
you

you are . . .

the water

that
is what I see

you
are the water . . .

empty blather
and
mere words

the soothsayer
may look –
she can
prophesy –
as much as she wishes
but
he is not listening

hears only
the wash of foam
racing
up the sand
of a lonely beach

that
is the future
he can *feel*

a staggered song (in three parts)

the sea

the sand

the streets

empty
teeming
oceans . . .

the music
of the deep
plays

a voice
in the breeze
sings
as well

there is a haunting
emptiness
in each
that is vocalized

a combination
of wind
and of whale

susurration
in two parts

and it sings
in the mind
of a seafarer
marooned

parted from his
vessel

his ocean

the albatross
that hovered above . . .

astern

parted
from his reason

in the night –
a gut full
of gut-rot –
he raises
his voice

a lament
for all
that ever
was
a lament
for all
that has ever
been

a lament
for himself
and for the end
of all the things

three parts
three voices
raised

a whistle
and a hum
and a man
calling
to the night
for release

a low-sung
song
of release

before he staggers
away

huge white (empty)

the tendril
is . . .

a leading finger

a beckoning

fog
and mist
encase the mind
of the man

he is not
thinking
but . . .

longing

responding

reacting

he is –
sometimes –
sounding

being
of the wyrd
of a huge white . . .

something

the fog
suggests
but does not reveal

will not
confirm

it is a huge
white . . .

it is an emptiness
that includes
a mariner
and
a man

water air ocean mother (at last)

the side
of a wave
is sheer

so straight a man
can fall . . .

plunge

from water
through air
into ocean

fall
to his doom
or . . .

salvation
may come

it takes many forms

a twisting
and convoluted
thing

that might catch
or
let fall

the lost
do not care

not
in that moment

over is –
after all –
over

the air
is deep

the ocean
fluid

and the waters will part
to make room
for the descendant

or . . .

it will not

there is a sound
of sibilance
and
of *shushes*

a sound –
too –
of bubbles

the deep
is green
before it turns
blue

before gray
and before night

it is
mother
to the child

and a kind of
cool
peacefulness

at last

ripples of a life (stilled)

he is
still

the waters
are moving

all
of his life

in ripples

still moments
wavering
before him . . .

fading

unremarkable
except for the fact
they are
his life

not
a very good
life

not
so terribly bad
either

a life lived

driven
by the tides

swirled
in eddies

spent
in pursuit
of a vision

a dream
perhaps

a compulsion toward
a completion
he did not know
that he lacked

he is
stilled
in the water

in the womb
of the mother

and all his life
is reborn
in a slow current
drifting past

dream a dream (swimming)

is it life . . .

being underwater?

how
does a man
breathe?

perhaps
he doesn't
and
perhaps he isn't

but
it *feels* as though
he is

suspended
above the ocean floor

moving arms
and legs
to propel himself –
to *swim* –
raising eddies of brown
and glint
from the sand
as he moves

fish
are loud creatures

there is sound
when they
swim

they can be heard
eating

chewing morsels

crunching coral

worms
in hollow tubes
hide
in their self-made
depths

anemones tickle
and retreat

tentacularly grasping
small prey

schools swish
in synchronised twists
and turns

this way . . .
that

eluding
the big vibration
that glides past
all open smile
and razored teeth

a man can swim
in this place

unaware
he is doing so

uncertain
if he is really
here
or dreaming

deep knowledge (and a sure dream)

there are pale tracts
of emptiness
illuminated poorly
by filter-light

pallid
and used up many times
before a dawdled arrival
at the sandy bottom
of this reach
of sea

so like
and so *un*-like
the hot desert
above

the great expanse
of nothingness
in which the whale
died

the ocean bed
is a place
of extremes

of life
and death

ennui
and danger

but no . . .

there is no
real
danger

he is protected
as he swims
down here
in the deeps

as he becomes
a part of this
greater whole

he has a shadow
swimming nearby –
just beyond
sight –
casting a protective
shade

and the sure knowledge
that this
is a dream

it is enough
and he will come
to no
harm

a song in seagrass (holy is the light)

the seagrass
washes
forward . . .

and back . . .

on the motion
of wave currents

it is a kind
of kelp-dance

there is a song
sung
on the ocean floor
that is all
sway
and implication

a pallid mariner
also sways

also dances

suspended mid-water
with his beard
and hair
streaming
the song
he
and the forest
of kelp
as one

light
from above
is also
suspended

rays emanating
from an implied
sun

spread out
and down
below a blur-edged
central orb

more white
than golden

the crooning man
is bathed
in soft light

dappled
in the dance

truly
he is nearing
a confrontation –
of sorts –
with purity

but
for *this* moment
the song
is implied –
only implied –
in the sway
of seagrass

the nature of a relic
(leviathan)

forget
all that

just
for a moment

consider the nature
of a shrine

a location
for relics

sainted relics

but
what
is a saint?

do we discuss
religion now . . .

belief . . .

the spirit . . .

what comprises
a relic

of *worth?*

and
is it a thing
to be
worshipped

what spirit
remains

to receive
such obeisance
in a scatter
of white ribs
that were –
once –

leviathan

whale bone (swim trembling)

does the water
tremble
beneath your girth
old fish?

no
no longer

it is only
your bones
that it must bear
now

ribs
and skull

scattered segments
of a tail

all cast about
by the tides
until unrecognizable
but . . .

I see you
old whale

I feel you
as a throb –
a current –
running
through the water

they are yours
yet
and they tremble

all the fishes tremble

for there is none
mightier
than the white
sperm whale

be at peace
old thing

old friend

at peace

a day comes

we will swim
together

the white whale
and I

when the lost pod sings (to sea again)

the mariners –
old whale-men all –
gather

perched
on makeshift stools

squatting
or simply
on the ground
with their backs
against a wall

these men
have known hardship
at the whim
of oceans
and are not above
a seat
upon the steady earth

their hands
are a devilish rainbow
of lined weather
black pitch
and the golden-brown
of foul-bac
smoked
or chewed

    spat

there is little left
for these men
now the whales
have gone

it is long
since a sighting
and their work
is reduced . . .

tying knots

mending nets
and tackle
for the sake of it

without real hope
of need

tale-telling liars –
these seamen –
but
if not a yarn
that brings to mind
the high seas . . .

what
is there?

and the story
has been told –
no one knows
who told it first –
about a mighty pod
of whales

the lost pod
they are calling them

whether
they are all
together
all the time
or come together
only in response
to some calling
of their wild
it is not said

but –
somehow –
it is known
that they come together . . .

they *will*
come together

to sing

some say
it is to mark
a new-born

the birthing
of a special calf

some say it is more
a *spiritual* thing
and all of the men
nod

they know
that the world of the whale
is a spiritual thing

others say it is a lie

that no man
has seen
such a thing

a *story* . . .

only
a story

but these last
are shouted down

for what does it matter
if it is just
a story?

stories
can be true

truer
than true

and they argue
on
and on
but . . .

in their secret
hearts

these black-handed men
of the sea
believe

and they wait –
each
with a hidden hope –

that the lost pod
will sing

that there will be
a special calf
or a special song

that the whales
will reappear

and the emptiness
of their
poor
land-locked lives
will fall behind

as their search
begins
again

a bristle (that smells like rum)

on the shore
a shaky man

wearing bristle
on his cheek
in the flavor
of cheap rum

the sound of it
is a raspy
grating

too loud
and too close

loose-leaf and foul
he rolls
a smoking stick

too fat
in the middle

as they always
are

extracts two
loose strands
with his lips
and teeth
spits them away
before striking
a lucifer

cups his hand
to draw
from the flame

once

twice

gazes
through his personal
atmosphere
out
to the distance
of salt water

every atom
of his being
senses the weather

a storm at sea
away
out there

water
crashing the deck

bare feet
attempting
to grip
the decking
while attending
to salvation

he can feel
what is coming
and recall
what it was

a freshening breeze
flirts
with a loose strand
of salt coloured
hair

salt water
salt hair

old salt

as a distant mountain
of cloud
discharges lightning
to boil and fizz
in the water
he wonders

> *will he ever again*
> *find a deck*
> *on which to stand*
> *in a storm?*

> *will the old world*
> *ever*
> *drift back within reach*
> *again?*

> *will the whale*
> *return*
> *to give meaning*
> *to lives*
> *stranded*
> *within a dream*
> *of what they were?*

he rasps
the rum smell
of his stubble
again

turns his back
to seek
another flagon

in the end . . . (a beginning)

there are questions
to be asked
about the whale

the nature
of it

how
it came to be
in a desert?

how it lived
so long
as it did?

did the ocean
dry
leaving it
stranded in
non-water?

did it stumble
in its wanderings . . .

first to beach
then to sand
then
the desert?

an accident
of sorts

was it a deliberate
decision
to sail in new seas

to feel the rasp
of non-water
against its skin?

or
is it just a way
to die?

one more way
to death

too weary to swim
anymore

pursued
by the mariner
until death –
outside of its element –
was preferable
to going on
in the same ways

.
.
.

or perhaps
there was
a call

something
that only the whale itself
could hear

that drew it
on

beyond merely beaching itself
on a shoreline
but . . .

being

in the non-place
that would
ultimately
claim it

perhaps
it somehow knew
that the time had come
for the mariner
too
the end
of one thing
so often
is the beginning
of another

is it not?

yonder (thunder weeps)

thunder weeps

did you know?

it rages
and rampages

grumbles
and growls

builds tension
to a point
you don't think
you can bear

certainly
the thunder
cannot bear it

eventually
it weeps

rain
in torrents
lashing the mountains
and the plains
the same

filling the ocean
where
it might have lost a drop
in its ceaseless
agitations

the ocean
doesn't mind

doesn't seem to care
or even to notice

she holds
her own counsel

accepts
the teardrop gifts
that the thunder
lets fall

but does not anger
unless the wind . . .

unless
the storm

then –
oh then –
she might rage

down
near the ocean floor

the sea-bottom –
a learning creature –
absorbs

yes
absorbs
the knowledge

perhaps
this is the way
in which a fish
might begin
to breathe . . .

breathing the air
of knowledge
from the ocean
and through the waters
of the sea

absorbing all
that there is to know
of the weeping
of thunder

away yonder
above the peaks
of mountains

what they say (about transformation)

there is a point
in the process
of transformation

a *tipping* point

one further
millimeter
of thought becomes . . .

the thought
of no return

step back
one millimeter . . .

the opportunity
lost

it is tense
this moment . . .

frightening
and thrilling

waiting for a sign
but –
possibly –
not needing it

knowing that
in the deeps
the power to act resides
if you *will* it . . .

one millimeter

in the meantime
you are
nowhere

nothing

floating

suspended
between being
and . . .

not

   speak

   *for god's sake say
   something*

it is a scream
but
none can hear it
a scream
burned within
the mind

they say
transformation
is
a terrible thing . . .

that
is what
they *say*

what is the worth (of everything)

beyond the urgency

beyond
the pursuit

what
was the heart . . .

the *core?*

what
was the driver?

reflections –
like flotsam –
drift by

questions
brought on
by stillness

action
replaced by thought

the driver
was *desire*

the heart
was a *need*

the pursuit
was a *path* –
a way to fill
an emptiness
of the self

and what
of success?

what of that moment
of accomplishment
when the pursuit
was finally
over?

it lay there –
dying –
in the sand

the elusive
finally attained
but only
as the death
of a dream

did we ask
about the dream?

no . . .

well
we can ask
now

what
was the dream?

was it worth
everything?

blood changes (forever)

what
is the difference
between the blood
of a whale
and that of a man?

is mammalia
in common
enough
to establish a kinship
bond?

could the one
be poured
into another?

perhaps blood
is the wrong
reference point

maybe
the kinship factor
is shown
in the physical

the flesh
and the bones

skin
and eyes
and fingers and limbs

mother-milk
and warm pulsation
of the heart

transcendental
more likely

minds reaching
through a void

touching
one another –
a *spiritual* thing –
like finding
god
by coincidence

sharing a void
with you

ichor
in the outer reaches

touched once

felt
once
pulsed
only once

changed
forever

failure to understand (the song is a mystery)

what
is the impulse
to kill?

the question
floats
as an unresolved
swirl
of current

for there *was*
such a moment

a first
sudden
up-swelling of impulse
to strike

deep into blubber
and flesh
with the harpoon

to seize and cease
a life
through the power
of personal desire

a heart-thumping
headiness
of panted breath
and giddiness

that the first attempt
failed –
a missed strike –
is of no import

the taste
of that desire
could never
be forgotten

not through all
the pursuits
that followed

until
death by other means
brought the sobering
of a slapped face
and the release
of a multitude
of personal
revelations
and realisations

a single moment
of impulsiveness
to rule
dictatorially
over an entire life . . .

two
entire lives

it is beyond
understanding

yet
the song of the whale
is deep
and filled
with its own
meanings

not love (until)

and
there is *love*

don't ask
what
that might be

know
that the heart
of desire

the essence
of that attraction
is *love*

the nature
of the pursuit?

chemistry . . .

perhaps

it is a chemistry of
first glimpses
then

a chemistry of
once
for a lifetime

and the realization
of loss
in its so many
forms

physical presence
and mental guide

stabilizing influence

all part
of the same wheel
turned down
at last

the weight
of a complete history

brought to bear
on the low point
of spoke
and rim

of course
there is . . .

there *was*
love

though
between us
we never
spoke of it
until

a wash of waves (and weaving)

all those things

those . . .

events
happened

they
were real

so real
there was no room
for anything else
in the space –
the *time* –
surrounding them

they were

life

as it was

especially
in the moment
when they were
committed

so real

the only
real

and now
they are marvels
that have the patina
covering
of an old image –
a painting

or
a photograph –
glimpsed
on a wall
or
pasted
into an album

a fading marvel

there is no
time
for them
now

no capacity
to bring them
back
into life

the waves
that washed clean –
or

washed dirty –
have gone

receded
on a tide
of life
and
of change

they have become –
fabric –
no more

the cloth
to be used
in new weaving

and as each image
skitters
to be
front of mind
for a moment
it is taken

absorbed
into the new
creature
striving to *become*

there are new
memories
waiting to be made
but
in the meantime . . .

the waves
and the weaving
do not
pause

testament in blue (for the executor)

is it time
then

for a last
will?

the testament?

very well
very well

let the body
that *was*
be washed
thoroughly and
through
all the seas
that surround the earth

let the mind
at last
be changed

let all that was
be
only that which
was

let the treasures
remain
as memories
to drift

occasionally
wrapping round
some unsuspecting soul
swimming

through the ocean
of one
once-upon-a-time

and may they be
the happy ones

the simple ones
the young

the carefree

as for
the rest . . .

as
for the rest . . .

may they transform
from grit
to sand
may they line
the beaches and
the deep
sea beds

underfoot
not
in the mind
where the chances are
of interference

let them be
where
they can cause no
interference

beyond that . . .

nothing

I have nothing
more

you will find me –
my testament –
somewhere
in the blue

love (possibly)

and is it not
true
that
the whale could
have swum . . .

anywhere?

could have left
the mariner
and his obsessions . . .

those fractured dreams
behind
at any time?

oh yes

it had
the strength
and
the power

it could have
accelerated
or
dived –
lord
how it could
dive –
and left him

why . . .

why
did it not
do that?

why
would it not
save itself
from the petty
pursuit?

perhaps
it was bound
to him

yes
that is possible

but
do you never wonder
at the role played
by . . .

what?

empathy
perhaps

a recognition
by the creature
of the mariner's need

maybe that
is too big
a stretch

perhaps
it exceeds
credible bounds

but the thought
persists

why did not
the creature who *could*
leave?

why allow
its own persecution?

truly
in this wide world
in
this vastness
that is a universe

there is love

for what else
could it
possibly
be?

moving (to scratch an itch)

the easier thing
is to stay –
to remain

it is harder
to become

to evolve into
the next
self

yet
to remain
carries a cost

personal evolution
is a restless thing

emergence demands . . .

energy
effort
involvement

choice

stasis –
on the other hand –
is a place
of comfort

of comfortable
regret

these are thoughts
that bring an itch
into consciousness

that force
a response

whether to deliberately
ignore it
no matter
the discomfort

or . . .

to scratch

.

.

.

the suspended mariner
bathed
in surrounding song
begins
to move

release (withing a singular breath)

is it
necessary
to change a thought . . .

all thoughts?

.

.

.

to alter
the position and stance
of the body
perhaps?

.

.

.

to fly
instead
of walking?

.

.

.

to swim?

.

.

.

perhaps all
of these things
at once . . .

sometimes
waiting is –
in itself –
a precursor
so . . .

wait

every thought
is a *doing*

each
bringing of something –
a *possibility* –
into consideration

there is no peace
in this thinking

only disturbance

distress

turmoil

a deep breath –
a *sigh* –
brings a small sense
of relaxation

an easing
of the muscles

settling
of the bones
properly
into their bodily
spaces

release –
a exhaled loosing –
of calm
and
the momentary cessation
of thought

not *thinking*
not *acting*
not *doing*
not . . .

just *being*

.

.

.

and
the next thought comes
a little
more easily

new light (shines bigger)

the song
is an insistent
thing

there is a demand
in the chords

within the notes

sound
penetrates
and there is no
avoiding
even if
there was a will
to do so

a time comes
when it is necessary
to confront
by embracing

to conquer
by absorbing

inhaling

osmosing . . .

and changing
with

it is no longer
a struggle
but more
an enlarging

a life
becoming

something bigger
in the light

a new light

noted (a new song)

listen
a moment

do you hear
the sound of birds?

of waves?

the surface
of some ocean
vibrant
and alive?

listen . . .

what
would it be like
to rise

to break
the surface

up

into the air

to exhale
spume
and inhale good air
again

free
and un-trapped
in old skin

old persona

to rise
completely
from the water

and smack down

and smack . . .

down

for sheer
joy?

it is
an academic
thought

idly occurring
but . . .

it needn't be

that
is the new element –
this knowledge –
it needn't be

there is coming
a sense
of size
and
of potential
and
of capacity
to *do* . . .

whatever is needed
to be done

a note
within the song
has changed

deep water (and a feeling)

and
at a point –
along
the line –
an opportunity
arises . . .

is sensed

do you not feel
that way . . .

do you never
stop

sniff the air

look around
to discover what
just happened . . .

what occurred?

it is the crossing
of a decision point

a marker
between what
was
and what
may be

an instant
of opportunity

a *diem*
to *carpe*

it is a powerful
moment

and a realization

whatever
is the response
nothing
will ever be the same
after

there is a rippling
in the sound
of the song
that can be
felt
through deep water

rising (as from sleep)

sleep
is a perpendicular
activity

seabed below

tail down

nose pointed
up
to the place
where light
from that distant sun
will begin
to filter down

it is
a stasis
of existence

a *waiting* time

the pod
surrounds the sleeper
sends a waking song
into the waters

into the body

the belly

the heart . . .

which beats
a slow drum

an emanating
confirmation
of life

the drum
beats

the tail
trembles

the whole
of the massive body
trembles

nd an eye
opens
to the first arrowing
of light
from above

the pod sings

the light
plays
a dapple

and the waters
allow

sleep
is a perpendicular
activity
and the way
to rise . . .

the *path*
to rising
is known

joy (is sung)

the prelude
to waking
is joy

that
is the sound

it is
the feeling

it is the first
awareness

the sensation
of *being*
within the correct
element

of being . . .

elemental

and
of being surrounded
by the love
of
an ocean

the pod
that sings
to awaken

and the song
that is
joy

with mighty thrusts (the bubbles rise)

it is
a mighty instrument

one impulse

one thrust

and the great creature
is moving

propelling itself
upward
to the source
of dapple
and filter light

upward
to beyond this element
of salted water

upward
to the air

a mighty thrust

a mighty
thrust

a
mighty

mighty

thrust

leaving only bubbles
to rise
at their leisure

a kind of following
shadow
of the leviathan

almost inaudible (the wheel turns)

from the desert
to
the sea

the mysterious vastness
to the vast
mystery

all of life
is
a cycle

and every wheel must
turn

it is not
a choice
but lies within
its nature –
within its very
wheel-ness –
to do so

each turn
reveals
a novel-ness
of aspect

a new facet

from the desert
to the sea

opposing vastness

competitive mystery

all
mere turns
of the wheel

~

on the derelict pier
looking out
across the water

a grizzled sailor
has fixed his eyes
on a storm

away off
toward the horizon

there is a colour
and
a sensation
that speaks of
portent
and he cannot
shift
his gaze

something
is occurring
and the glass
is dropping
as though
for storm

as though
for typhoon
or hurricane

as though . . .

something
is coming

and with each
falling
millibar
the feeling of oppressive
expectation
rises

with it the
almost inaudible sound
of a whale
singing

one is (one was)

what
is left
after transformation?

the cicada
leaves behind
a brown husk

an avatar
of what
it may have looked like
had it never
changed

what
of a man?

a stick figure
outline
drawn
onto damp sand?

waiting

waiting
for a rise
in the tide
to take it away

erase
or carry off

there is little
difference
for the *man*
is gone

he will not return

he is . . .

become
something *other*

and he swims
with a giant eye
open

to see what there is

what *new*
there is

the tide
is a whisper
as it carries him
grain by grain
into
the one
that is now

was a life (refined)

is it
easy
do you think . . .

this process
of transformation?

no

only
the untransformed
could believe that

being
not being

being again

simple enough
to precis

but
fire burns

we talk of
husks
and old selves
left behind
as though a wriggle
is enough
to free the future
from the past

but
fire burns

to death

burns to life

and the new
is raw

painful

tender

and
stronger

more refined

more resilient

powerful
and complete

all true
but never forget
the fire burns
and the debris –
the *detritus* –
left behind . . .

unrecognizable
though it may be

was a life

a song (of senses)

this is
a journey
to find your voice

through all the seasons
of your life –
until now –
you have been
silent

yes
we heard you

yes
you heard yourself
and spoke aloud

yes
yes

but now
you must find
your voice

not
words uttered
and
blandishments offered
or curses
thrown in frustration

no

this is the voice
to still
your longings

to realise
your desires

this is the voice
with which
you will sing the song
to still
all of the world
that has ears
to hear

as you rise
through the waters
look within

find
the sound
of yourself
that waits

use your senses

sing

gone (as grit)

is there
merit
at this late stage

in an inspection
of the ruin
of a life . . .?

perhaps

perhaps not

much can be learnt
of course
but . . .

that creature died

what *was*
is no guide
to what
is

will you recognize
the one
when gazing
upon the other?

that creature
is reborn
and
is new

still red
still raw
from
the cauterization

leave
the old carcass
to lie

to be washed
and disbursed
by the fickle tides

to be
gone
as grit
to the ocean

disconnected bubbles (are the past)

a great creature
rises

almost
it has become
what it now
must be

all that remains
are a few
disconnected bubbles
of thought

flashes
in the colours worn
by old memories
that cling
tenaciously

the rest –
all of it –
is new

is waiting

is next

the sensations
of movement
through the water
propelled upwards
thrust

by mighty
thrust
is . . .

magnificent

waters part

there is no place
no time
for any more
than this
scant awareness
of a past

a history
and
an already lived
moment

thrust –
the mighty tail –
thrust

rise

what story (what ending)

what story
is this?

the mariner . . .?

the whale . . .?

neither?

yes
perhaps neither

more
maybe
it is of death

the little death
of a spirit
mortally wounded

more again –
perhaps –
it is of birth

despite everything

what story
are you hearing
told
in the old
sailor tradition . . .

told
as a toast
at the funeral

spoken
in wonder
at the first glimpse
of a sleeping new-born

sung
as a legendary mystery

by a traveling troubadour
in return for the jangle
of a penny
striking the bottom
of his tin cup?

think now
before the imminent end
what story is this
that you
are hearing?

heedless a slap (is coming)

the pier
and the shoreline
are lined
shoulder to shoulder

none
will fish
today

the ocean –
toward the horizon –
is . . .

forbidding

expectant

first one
grizzled old saltwater
deckman

then . . .

more

silently assembled

men
of the water
and
who know the deep –
as only hunters
and lovers can –

will not go forth
today

but watch
from the shore

there is a storm
of cloud
complete
with flashes
as of lightning

there is a circle –
an *outer* circle –
that is the grey
of murky deeps

the water
is all chop and surge
and swell

wave mountains
with white caps

and
there is blue

a heart
of blue

a circle of calm

illuminated by shafts of sun
bursting through
the overhanging
dismay

every eye
is drawn
to the blue
even as the spray
carries a slap
of damp significance
with which to smite them

awe-struck
on the shore

they watch
heedless

waiting

on the surface (wild again)

the surface
is near
now

the trajectory
is direct

a ripple
of disconsonance
precedes the creature
in its rise

high

it leaps
from water
into air

into sunlight
and blue

leaps
and turns

then *smashes*
back
onto the surface

dispersing it
drop by drop
and foaming splash
by foaming splash
to send the word

and all around –
at the edges
of the sheltered circle
of blue water –
the pod
exhales

a song
of birth
within the spray
that is a combination
of water and air
and life

the *slap*
of landing
signals the end
of a beginning

and the high seas
and wild winds
are released
to run
as they will

the pod
is gone

the surface
is wild
and free
again

new orders (fateful days)

it is a
fateful
day

the wind
carries the message

    today . . .

    today . . .

there is a boat –
a small thing
of little weight
and
no consequence –
alone
on the heaving waters

thrown
this way and that
at the whim
of the saltwater
gods

bobbing
like a discarded cork
with all hands
scrambling
striving

praying
for deliverance
from a fateful
day

the captain
is at the helm

steady

eyes fixed
on the rolling
tumbling
waves

his boat
rises
atop a mountain

a fateful day

he glimpses . .

thinks
he has glimpsed
another wave
just as mountainous

thinks
he has seen

something . . .

   large

   white

   a whale

he thinks

he has not seen
its like
before
but . . .

he *knows* it

it is
his

his whale

and he knows
with all his heart
with
all his life
that he must
hunt it
chase

pursue

capture

he has to have it

the wave
subsides
and from within
a grey trough
within the relentless waters
he opens his mouth
to shout

there are new
orders
to be issued

Author Information

About the Author

Frank Prem has been a storytelling poet since his teenage years. He has been a psychiatric nurse through all of his professional career, which now exceeds forty years.

He has been published in magazines, online zines, and anthologies in Australia, and in a number of other countries, and has both performed and recorded his work as spoken word.

He lives with his wife in the beautiful township of Beechworth in North East Victoria, Australia.

Connect with Frank

As the author, I hope you enjoyed this volume of poetry collection. I think that mine is a unique style of writing that can appeal well beyond a 'pure poetry' readership.

If you enjoyed it, I'd like to ask you to do two small things for me.

First leave a short review of this book with your preferred online retailer by visiting White Whale Universal link and following it to your preferred online retailer leaving a customer review of the book.

Online reviews provide social proof to readers and are critical to Indie authors such as myself.

The second thing is, please pop over to my author page www.FrankPrem.com, and subscribe to receive my occasional Newsletter.

From time to time I'll let you know what is happening with myself and my writing, as well as keeping you informed of any giveaways I may be planning.

You can also find me on Facebook, Twitter, Instagram and YouTube.

Other Published Works

Free Verse Poetry

Small Town Kid (2018)

Devil In The Wind (2019)

The New Asylum (2019)

Herja, Devastation - With Cage Dunn (2019)

Walk Away Silver Heart (2020)

A Kiss for the Worthy (2020)

Rescue and Redemption (2020)

Pebbles to Poems (2020)

The Garden Black (2022)

A Specialist at The Recycled Heart (2022)

Ida: Searching for The Jazz Baby (2023)

From Volyn to Kherson (2023)

Alive Is What You Feel (2023)

Picture Poetry/Spoken Image

Voices (In The Trash) (2020)

The Beechworth Bakery Bears (2021)

Sheep On The Somme (2021)

Waiting For Frank-Bear (2021)

A Lake Sambell Walk (2021)

A Few Places Near Home (2023)

What Readers Say

Small Town Kid

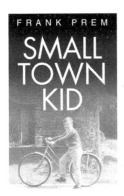

A modern-day minstrel

Small-Town Kid is a wonderful collection

—S. T. (Australia)

A poet's walk through his childhood in a small Australian town.

—J. L. (USA)

Devil In The Wind

Instantly grips you by the throat in his step-by-step story of survival.

Bravo!

—K. K. (USA)

Outstanding!

—B. T. (Australia)

The New Asylum

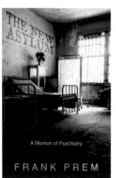

Words can't do justice to the emotional journey I travelled in (reading this collection).

__C. D. (Australia)

If I had to pick one book over the past year that has truly resonated with me, this would be it.

__K. B. (USA)

Walk Away Silver Heart

Has an extraordinary way with words and his poems invoke great passion and emotion in the reader.

—R C (United States)

As Memorable as My Favourite Music

—M D (United States)

A Kiss For The Worthy

A Celebration of Life Written in Thoughtful Bursts of Poetic Expression

—C M C (United States)

With every verse, I found myself reflecting about myself, my life, and the world.

—K

Rescue and Redemption

The passion of love in its many forms explored by one for another.

—J L (United States)

I've enjoyed every word, every breath. Every moment within the life of these stories.

—C D (Australia)

Sheep On The Somme

Museums and archivists take note-- sell this in your gift shops, preserve it in your archives. Professors, teachers- -share with your students.

—A R C (United States)

(This) book is a beautiful and graphic tribute to all those brave men and women who gave their lives for their countries between 1914 and 1918.

—R C (South Africa)

Ida: Searching for The Jazz Baby

I found myself deeply moved by the presentation of Ida's elusive, illusionary life.

—E G (United States)

He gives her a depth and vulnerability that the press didn't.

— A C (United Kingdom

The Garden Black

THE
GARDEN BLACK

and other speculations

FRANK PREM

Prem creates verse that illuminates our world, its experiences and history.
—S C (United Kingdom)

Prem's poetry reminds that life is fragile and fleeting ... both harsh and beautiful.

—D G K (United States)

Herja, Devastation

Herja,
Devastation

Frank Prem &
Cage Dunn

Simply written, powerfully felt. __C. (Australia)

As a combination of poetry, prose, and wonderfully ominous illustrations, I found Herja, Devastation refreshingly original. Highly recommended!

—G. B. (Australia)

Bravo! Outstanding!

—B. T. (Australia)

Index of Poems

A

a bristle (that smells like rum) 89
a feeling foreseen (in the foam) 61
almost inaudible (the wheel turns) 136
a song in seagrass (holy is the light) 78
a song (of senses) 143
a splash (of whale water) 39
a staggered song (in three parts) 63
a swim light (an ocean destiny) 57
a wash of waves (and weaving) 110

B

blood changes (forever) 103

D

deep knowledge (and a sure dream) 76
deep water (and a feeling) 129
disconnected bubbles (are the past) 147
dream a dream (swimming) 73
drowning perhaps (never alone) 44

E

edges shaved (throbbing on) 54
encouragement (at an ending) 13

F

failure to understand (the song is a mystery) 105

G

gone (as grit) 145
grief or glee (a whipping) 33
ground sung (the ocean) 58

H

heedless a slap (is coming) 151
huge white (empty) 66

T

W

Y

www.FrankPrem.com

Milton Keynes UK
Ingram Content Group UK Ltd.
UKHW020848220224
438295UK00014B/488